The Black Male Teacher Experience

Willie Williams Jr.

Copyright © 2017 Willie Williams Jr.
All rights reserved.
ISBN-10:1977915949
ISBN-13:9781977915948

DEDICATION

Dedicated to all the Black teachers who understand what the struggle is.

CONTENTS

1	Beginning of the Year
2	What will make our black boys learn
3	Physical Presence of a Pharaoh
4	White Woman's Race
5	Dear Parents
6	Black Batman
7	Villain Tales
8	You need to step it up?
9	Prayer to Testing
10	209 Tunes Part one

11	Do Not Hire List
12	3 Girls Hugged Me
13	We Heard You Were Leaving
14	No Safety Help
15	To the Black Girl Students
16	Gradebook
17	A Bug Can Break A Military
18	They are What they eat
19	Frustration Point
20	Another Black Male Teacher…
21	Man Syndrome
22	Won't Be Teaching Long
23	Where's the Justice?
24	Brown Eyes Watching
25	209 Tunes Part Two
26	Black Male Teaching Commercial
27	Honesty Break
28	Ya'll the reason why I've sick
29	You are eleven, but we expect you to be 31
30	Black Unicorn

FOREWORD

I have the privilege of working in the greatest profession any human can ever endeavor to practice. In no way am I overlooking or degrading other professions, however I truly appreciate mine. Doctors are tasked with giving us the best practices of staying healthy and improving quality of life when we are sick. They are definitely important. Lawyers are tasked with protecting our legal rights and bringing those to justice who have violated them. Masons, carpenters, electricians, plumbers, HVAC specialist, roofers, etc. are tasked with how efficient and comfortable our homes will be.

In my profession I am tasked with training and managing the future creators of culture, industry and ingenuity. I must teach them values that will teach them from venturing on the other side of "no, don't do it". I will teach them **to learn from the mistakes of others instead of repeating the mistakes of others.** I must teach them to have love for their fellow man even when they do not have love for themselves. Being a school teacher is more than teaching a scholar their abc's and 123's. It's about teaching moral and values. However, I cannot just teach it, I must model it. Every day I must exemplify what it is to be a righteous human being. When parents call or come by irritated and agitated because their scholar came home with a bad grade. I have to stay focused when my colleagues and front office staff do not approve of my teaching style. Not because it is wrong, but because it is different from their own. Throughout all of the disrespect and frustrations that cause sleepless nights I will continue to walk into my school every morning, on time, with a smile on my face because I know that kids who look like me need to see someone who looks like them. Genuinely displaying what it means to be a black man.

This is my task, my job, my profession and possibly my obsession. I have been trusted with the greatest commodity on our planet which is our children, our Future.

-Jermaine Dunlap

Beginning of the Year

It is the beginning of the school year
    and you can feel the excitement
    The anxiousness
    The uneasiness
    Kids who hate that their summer ended
    Teachers who are anxious to meet the students
    who they heard about
    read data about
    been warned about
    The day starts and everyone is anxious
    Students ready to learn
    and ready to test you
    who don't know you
    They don't know how hard you worked to get to that very position
    How hard you studied
    acted white
    acted like you were the smartest in the room

Just for the opportunity to be in front of them

To counter you don't know how hard they worked
How hard they faked to like the last teacher
How much trauma they have been through
How much they have cheated and grinded
Just for the opportunity to be in front of you
The bell rings
and the struggle begins

Amin

What will make our black boys learn?

First off,
    We've been learning
    See our lives are about survival
    So we learn how to protect ourselves at all cost
    to keep our hands on the steering wheel
    and to keep our mouths shut to not conflict
    We learn about sports to free us from our under resourced communities
    Learn about women to free us from the pressures of life
    Learn about the systems around us to free us from unintentional mishaps
    Our black boys learn alot
    But since you asked,

    Our Demands:

Curriculum that's about us instead of lifeless standards & language we don't
   use

Black Teachers who understand what life looks like for Black students

Black Male Teachers who understand what life looks like for Black Males

Systems in which we just don't have to comply to rules we did not set

A hand in creating these systems

To learn about who we are and what we have created

Math lessons about how the pyramids were built using perfect geometry

Science lessons about George Washington Carver use of chemistry

English lessons about our vernacular and how it transformed literature

History lessons about the Black Panthers and their resistance against the dominant narrative of whiteness

Teachers that learn about us
Teachers that do not fear us
Less being asked to sit in uncomfortable chairs for hours on end
Less being told to be quiet and to stop talking during those hours
Less questions about what will make us learn
More questions about what is in the way of our learning

So when you ask,
What will make us learn
Just know that every day we are
Although we might not show it on a test or in class
If you give me a de stressor like 2k Myplayer I can learn it real fast
We go through all these years of schooling and still get discriminated against

still get shot down in the street
   still get labeled dumb or not good enough
   even with a 4.0 GPA

   We have been learning all along
   and understand these concepts as well as math or reading

Physical Presence of a Pharaoh

Walking into the school like it is game seven of the NBA finals

    Beats Headphones block out all of the crowd noise

    I arrive at the school and begin my day

    Whenever I walk into somewhere the whole room stops

    Kids immediately notice my presence and decide whether they should speak

    Maybe it is because I am six feet tall

    or maybe it is because my inner Pharaoh is showing

    Walking into grade level meetings

    Laptop cradled in my arms

    I arrive to the meeting and begin my descent into my chair

    Again the whole rooms stops

    Fellow teachers immediately notice my presence and decide whether they should speak

Maybe it is because I walked in with a look of happiness and determination
or maybe it is because my inner Pharaoh is showing

Walking into the bathroom
Clipboard filled with names of students whom I both know and do not know
I arrive and begin to wash my hands
The room stops again
Students immediately notice my presence and decide whether they should speak
Maybe its because I walked in on business
or maybe my inner pharaoh is showing

My presence looms even when I do not
When I stand the whole room notices

Kids pay attention, even if they are in mid conversation

Their eyes burning a hole through me

I have arrived and my inner pharaoh is definitely showing.

White Woman's Race

I tie my shoes for the first time

    Ready to run for my country in the Olympic sprints of education

    Other racers hand out candy to the crowd, winning them over

    I stretch and say to remember a quote from a friend

    "I Know Why I'm Here" -Khalid El-Amin

    I put my feet on the line

    and look to the side and see others that do not look like me

    They smile and wave

    Knowing that they've been prepared and ran on this track many times before

    Knowing that I am a new runner and most of my people never make it this far

    The bell rings and we take off

    The crowd cheers for them, although I am a product of that very same crowd

I am confused, but vow to stay focus on the goal of winning

I run with a form that's mixed with the soul of my ancestors mixed with high education learned structure

I keep my head up, heart to God, face to the rising sun, and feet above the ground

I take long strides, while using my wait/weight to give me speed and force

I run like greyhounds are after my scent while I am navigating through swamp

I run like a violent mob is after me, wanting to tie me and watch me dangle

I run like a police officer is after me, with his gun draw, ready to fire

Running hard for my students

Approaching I can see the finish line, but I can also see the other runners too

Although they are not running for the same thing, they run well

Although they are not running from the same things, they run well

We are nearing the finish line as I prepare to propel head first

I am easily ahead of the other runners now

I stretch and feel tape whip across my face

Crossing the finish line with ease

I feel triumphant and magical

I won,

Right?

As the awards are handed out, my hands are left empty

When I ask about my award, I am looked at violently

"You actually have to run around the track twice"

"I'm not sure why you looked confused"

"You didn't know this?"

"They only have to do it once"

"So therefore you lost"

"If you want to win next time, maybe you should be more like them"

Dear Parents

Dear Parent,

I am writing to inform you that I am disappointed in you.

Your attendance has been subpar

with you barely showing up for meetings, conferences, and events.

You don't answer the phone because you do not want to be bothered

I mean you deal with them at home, but we need to come together

and you won't

I do not appreciate you just pawning your child off on me

and not even checking in once a week to see how they are doing

They miss you too and wish you were more involved

But you refuse to be

You do not even know what my classroom looks like

    You do not even know how I struggle with your child
        and still grow with them
        You just disappear out of existence
        then have the nerve to come complain
        What work have you done?
        You say you check your child's homework
        but I can tell that you did not
        You are subliminally telling your kid to not care about school
        because you do not care about it
        You just send them and tell them to "Be Good"
        without even looking at what "being good" in school takes
        and when you get upset you come and complain
        entering back into existence
        disturbing culture
        to prove your child's innocence

without even looking at the scene of the crime

    Why aren't you more active?
    Why do you not check homework?
    Why don't you call or email?
    Why won't you meet me halfway?
    Why haven't I seen you all school year?

    When will you become a parent for all 24 hours?

Black Batman

Here is a typical 24 hours at Unlucky Academy on the South East Side of Gotham:

    Bruce Wayne wakes up and gets ready for work

    Bruce Wayne arrives at work and everything is well and present

    Bruce Wayne cleans the boards and begins working

    The Joker arrives and starts creating panic amongst the other students

    Bruce Wayne sees that its time for Batman so he slips away to change

    The Joker completely ravages the school

    Batman arrives to save the day and mitigate the situation

    Batman however can not end the Joker though, that is against his morals

The Joker and Batman have an epic battle that destroys the classroom

Batman wins and hands the Joker over to the Police Chief

The Joker spends some time behind bars before

The Joker then tricks the Police Chief into letting him go

Instead calling Batman a hero, Batman is then called a Vigilante

Joker is freed and back in the classroom again

Joker lies low to keep a short profile for the day

Batman and The Joker go about their separate ways

Both knowing that the lost and won in the same day

The Joker lost the fight, but was cunning enough to escape discipline

Batman won the fight, but was labeled a vigilante who shouldn't take justice into his own hands

The Joker goes back to his clown gang to tell them the day
Batman drives home in his bat mobile

The next day the sun rises

Bruce Wayne wakes up and gets ready for work
Bruce Wayne arrives at work and everything is well and present
Bruce Wayne cleans the boards and begins working
The Joker arrives and starts creating panic amongst the other students

Villain Tales

I spend 85 percent of the day
    being someone who I did not come here to be
    I strut into school with a light attitude
    ready to fill minds
    and feel hearts
    but as soon as I walk in
    I realized that in order to succeed, I need to be someone else
    Here's the growing up on the westside theory again
    Act hard or get your chain snatched
    I have to be mean to students or get my name snatched
    Might as well be named Mr. Villain
    although I set out to be the hero
    I frown so much, I forget what smiling is like in here
    Yell so much, I forget what normal talking sounds like

 Oppress so much, I forgot I was here to free
 But what else do you do when surrounded by 37 young wolves
  who feed off each other
  and can tell whether they should try it or not in 15 seconds
  Get eaten or eat
  Villain Tales

You Need To Step It Up?

I'll first give you a classroom
    Put 24 low to middle level students in it
    Then close another classroom to give you 38 students
    I'll give you all the "problem kids" because you're a black man you know and that's what they need
    I'll give you a majority of the IEP students in case one of the Special Education teachers quit
    I'll give you the kids that everyone has on their "stay away list"
    I'll then change your lunch period
    Flip your schedule entirely
    Give you a scripted curriculum to where I only want you be "Teacher:"
    Curriculum that does not support the "testing" that you're measured heavily on

    Give you observations that are not full and don't get a glimpse of your actual classroom

    Yell at you about your 37 bodies making noise going up the stairs after recess

    Like 37 bodies anywhere can be quiet

    Degrade you and the work of your students

    Tell you that if you do not like it, there are 664 other schools you can go to

    I'll take away the teachers in the grade level with any experience

    Leaving you as a new teacher to flounder

    I'll then take every cry for help as criticism

    and I'll make sure I take it back out on you with petty emails about you, but addressed to all the staff

    I'll then change your lunch period again

Making sure your students don't eat until 2 pm after their only other meal was at 8:45

I'll chastise you for how you chastise your students

Because even though saying good morning before you enter the classroom is cute and teaches manners,

when they don't do it,

I then have to hear about it

I'll question how your test scores are what they are

If they are good, I'll question you like "What are you doing different?"

Fake love

If they are bad, I'll question you like "What are you doing different?"

"You need to step it up"

Prayer to Testing

Oh Great Test
Please Be Merciful with your wrath
    I come to you asking for good scores for my students
    I come asking for non biased reading of their writing
    I come to you begging to end your strangle on whether they are good enough or not
    I see that you make students either successes or failures
    Your one cold utterance of a score
    Can make a earth move...
    or a room shake with laughter...

    You know not these students hearts or what they go through every day
    But it is to you that they answer to

So I will make sure they are silent and do not disrespect you

Even if you are not in the room, I will mention your name to invoke fear and humility

I will even respect you

Thank you to the ones who made you

Who have never had a pizza puff or a Philly cheese steak,

but phrase questions around squash and chicken casserole ingredients

So if I can ask for anything:

Please be kind to my **Pear son's**

They do not have real **PARCCs**

They are descendants of **NWeA**

Even **ISAT** in a room like them before

They don't realize testing can capture you in **ANET**

Sometimes they don't know how to **ACT**
If only they would've just **SAT** quietly
If only they knew how to **ASK** for help

But they can't
Because you hear and see all
You are what growth is
You show us what we know and do not know
You tell us how smart we are
You Rein Supreme
Oh Testing
Please Be Merciful with your wrath

209 Tunes part one

We listen to music a lot

    How could we not with the ancestors of soul, blues, rock, and hip hop in the same room

    I take request mixed with playing selections of my own

    I play Complicated by Nivea for my girls

    They sing along to lyrics that are old as them

    and they feel them, bobbing their heads and dancing in their seats

    They don't understand how complicated this teaching thing is

    but I sing along in my head with them

    because things are complicated, you know

Next is Justfayu by Kamau
they dance to the African tribal beat
feeling their ancestors hum through pain
Meanwhile I sing the phrase
"I did it just for you, and you just don't care"
Knowing that I've been through all this and you don't care
they dance and clap
feel liberated from the chains of education
slaves in the fields dancing and clapping
celebrating the big house burning down

I take a request from a girl that has lost her mother at an early age
I'll be missing you be Diddy feat. Faith Evans plays through the speakers
I hear her sing the chorus

and have to stand outside the door because tears are forming
   the other students feel the vibe
   and even the meanest student says nothing about her singing
   as she sings for healing and understanding
   while singing she finishes all her work
   I am proud and terrified at how she deals with the trauma at the same time

   Dilemma by Nelly plays next
   and the young girls sing along
   they didn't grow up with the St. Lunatics
   but they feel the St. Louis aura and sing about love and acceptance
   Lives that they want and dream to have later
   Finding the meaning of love in the beat

There Goes My Baby followed by Dangerously in Love is next
   all request
   but timeless songs for students who don't have time on their side
   They don't try to be Usher or Beyonce
   but they sing with the passion of these singers

   I then play Crazy by K-Ci & JoJo
   we are vibin and learning now
   I tutor them on the first song to use auto tune
   They tutor me on how my song choices are old
   but they dance and learn along
   not knowing how crazy I go when I take a day off
   crazy to see them the next day

I then play my favorite classroom song
Always be my baby by Mariah Carey
the students know this one is for me
we all sing along
no longer singing in our heads
I point to students to let them know they will always be my students
always be in my hearts
always be the ones who I have countless stories about
They look at me weird
maybe they have never heard a black man sing about love and mean it
Mariah Carey didn't know she made this song about me and my 5th graders

We stop to get more academic work done
but we both know how much emotional work has been done in the process

Do Not Hire List

Being a teacher is not all it's cracked up to be
    I mean the easiest part is the kids
    and thats saying A LOT
    The hardest part is the adults
    Politics and Power now run the world of education
    creating new slavery systems of either comply
    or goodbye

    So just imagine a slave who goes to work everyday
    Although he loves the work he does
    He hates his masters and overseers,
    for they think he never brings in enough cotton

    They hate him
    He never praises them enough or shows joy in pleasing them

    He speaks up and plans for a revolution
    Peaceful, but permanent
    He also talks the other slaves into freeing their chains
    and running away to a better place
    Overhearing this,
    They devise a scheme to have him killed
    to protect their lies and cash in on the insurance policy
    They then go behind his back to the authorities
    with claims of mistreatment and disrespect
    They act like the whip was on their backs
    instead of in their hands
    The authorities come down upon the slave with the wrath of a God
    They beat him into self misery and doubt

They then place a mark on him
for everyone to see and know
for no one to ever plan a revolt again
even if folks wanted to help him, they couldn't
his new marking now states,
"DO NOT HIRE"

3 Girls Hugged Me

1...............2.............3..
    Then they swarmed me
    Wrapping their arms as tight as they could around me
    They formed a perfect triangle around me
    and hugged me for dear life
    Feelings of love, long-suffering, and longing
    defeating feelings of hate, hurt, and harassment
    3 girls hugged me at the end of the day
    Breathing deeply as if they were out of breath
    Breathing life into my soul
    Reminding me that my girls need love too

One a trouble maker that had never known her father
One a passionate fireball that lost her mother
One a younger sibling that was lost in the shuffle
They found love in the embrace

I, a male teacher that needed love and to be taught how to love
I, an adult that forgot what love is without returning something for it
I, a black soldier that felt appreciation and validation
I found true love of peace in their embrace

Their arms let me know it was full of understanding and credibility
Their shoulders let me know it was full of respect and admiration

Their hearts let me know they weren't the monsters that were described

I first screamed for them to let me go
Foolishly knowing I had to be overly strong in such a delicate situation
But they held tight knowing that it was needed
Wisdom dripping from their educated smiles

I then accepted they wouldn't let me go
Foolishly realizing that I couldn't be overly strong in such a delicate situation
As they held tight knowing it was needed
Wisdom dripping from my heart

They finally let go
and took my fears
hopelessness

and worries with them

They ran off as quick as they sacked me with the hug
and as I walked off
Full of love and happiness
One of my coworkers stated:
"Be careful about hugging the female students"
"You could get in trouble for that"
"You gotta be smarter about the type of interactions you have with your girls"

1....2...3....
My worries
Anguish
and misunderstanding
Were back again

We Heard You Were Leaving

Setting:
    Holiday Christmas Party

    They walk up with drinks and appetizers in their hands
        Using small talk at first to draw me in

        the "glad its the break" talk

        detailing how we need to be away from kids and how crazy they are
        saying how it's rough teaching in "the hood"
        and how these kids don't really "care about much"
        You know, teacher small talk

        Then they hit me with the main course
        this time cutting right to the chase

"So we heard you were leaving"
  my face immediately becomes stoic
  mind reminding me "You've been trained for this"
  I wonder a mixture of "Why do they care" and "Who sent them to ask this"
  I then grin and say "Well you know rumors are always present"
  Their faces remain intrigued
  With even a hint of caring in their eyes
  They begin to throw on the dressing of compliments
  "You know those kids really need you" "You are changing their lives"
  "They never had anyone stay" "They'd be devastated if you left"

  I begin to think about the students and how leaving would look

I begin to daydream dramatic grayscale images of students staring out the window while I drove away. Me sadly staring into the windshield, driving away from love and need. The students then sulking back to their...

"I know it might be rough, but you should stick it out"
I snapped right out of it
"Yeah I'll most likely be here with them, No Worries"
I turned around to get a plate
and out the corner of my eye, saw the same teachers who were asking
throw the principal a thumbs up

Scene

No Safety Help

Teaching is sometimes like being an NFL Corner

    With a good administration or defense, you will always have a safety over the top

    If you get beat, the safety is there to make the play

    or at least hit hard enough to jar the ball loose

    But with a less than adequate administration or defense, you will never have a safety over the top

    If you get beat, it's an automatic touchdown

    no one to hit hard, instead other fans cheering and laughing

    All corners get beat sometimes
    All teachers eventually burn out
    We all know this is true

    But when they have no safety help

teachers wonder why they are even playing
    You launch 38 students at me, and I defend all of them, but one or maybe two
    Which is actually a good average
    I should be getting paid millions
    I mean I keep students out the end zone for the most part
    But how can I possibly defend this many passes at once

    Comments are made about how I need to change my approach
    Need to start off pressing up against
    but have the ability to run with
    and keep my eye on the ball

    I try this way, but some students still make it to the end zone
    You then become frantic
    Upset and Overwhelmed

Acting as if we lost the super bowl every game
    You'd rather me get scored on
      then be on the student's highlight reel

To The Black Girl Students

Dear Beautiful Young Ladies,
    I am enamored with ya'll strength and positivity
    So I decided to write a letter expressing my love for you
    and in wanting to be both honest to my writing as well as you
    I will start with saying
    I love you
    I am strong enough to challenge society by saying such
    Even though I know some readers will misjudge my writing
    Making it something it is not
    Based on their own thoughts of non sexual love or lack of
    Any who
    I love you
    and I will scream it if I need to
    I love how
    Loud. Vibrant.

Mature. Quiet.
Loving. Demanding.
Attentive. Full of Energy.
You are
When I first came into the game
I wanted to save your counterparts
But I realize that my greatest joy comes from teaching you
Ya'll are so
strong and independent, so
brave and fearless, so
easily forgiving and thought provoking, so...
you
I love when you all stand up, united together
when the boys do you wrong
you stand and say, "I will not allow it"
Sounding just like your grandmothers and mothers before you
I love you all for that!

When the class gets too loud, you are my trumpets to silence

When a fight is about to happen, you are there to cool and separate

When I feel like I should quit, you write me a letter to say thank you

None of this is your job

but these are things you do out of the kindness of your heart

and I love you for that!

So thank you for your laughs

Your smiles, Your dancing, your intuition, your forgiveness, your screaming at the boys to open the door for you, for you

You all have taught me another layer to being a man

another layer to being a person

another layer to being a teacher

I appreciate you because you challenge me

You challenge yourself to not be what you see around you

You challenge the people around you to be better than they should be

You hold so much power in your hands

Yet you do not abuse it, instead you share it

Teaching would suck without you

Respectfully,
A Black Male Teacher

PS.
Instead of the Pledge of Allegiance, I should recite this to you all everyday. Wonder what would happen then?

Gradebook

Grades are due by Friday at 10 am
    and I've barely graded anything
    but I have to give you a grade
    so I sift through your assignments
    realizing that your sentences do not make sense
    I know from monitoring the classroom
    That you understand the material
    You paid attention
    Talked in groups about it
    ask questions during my teaching
    bought into learning
    But your sentences do not make sense
    too many grammatical errors, misspellings, not enough text evidence
    well correct text evidence
    So I grade it as I am supposed to do
    Grade the work and not the student

because if you learned, you should be demonstrate it
just as the standard says
Right?

So I give you an F on the assignment
and you look at me confused
you knew the content, but couldn't demonstrate it

You yell, "I shouldn't have even turned this in"
Frustrated because you tried
but Frustrated begins with a F and that's what you got

You instantly become disinvested
stop paying attention
start distracting groups
ask no questions during my teaching

no longer buying into the dream of learning
you are more concerned with the whooping that you will get at home
you now cut your eyes at me
put your head down
and sleep
dealing with the trauma of an unfair grading scale
the grading scale is 93-100 for an A
93-86 for a B
85-78 for a C
78-70 for a D
70 and under for an F

I think of it as a shame
if you got a 7 out of 10 on an assignment, you would still get an F
Meanwhile the growth between 93 and 100 is ironically 7 points

I know your parents won't understand how much hard work you put in
    they will see the F and be Furious accordingly
    so I watch you return the next day
    sliding sore into your seat
    and try again
    just to suffer the same result
    as I enter your F again
    What a Failure we are...

A Bug Can Break A Military

"THERE'S A BUG IN HERE!!!!"

The block scrams like gnats in the kitchen
    desk toppling like garbage cans in an alley
    the hardest ones on the block even run scared of one single B
    The same ones that just got ready to fight
    now hold on to each other for dear life
    There are some who choose to fight
    and some who chose flight

"ITS BY YOU!!!!!"

More panic as they point to the general
Fear in their eyes as they inch away

Like the person in front of them just got jumped on

The whole community is shaken

The bug is only trying to escape from the fear

trying to find the nearest window to remove themselves

but it is greeted with swats, swings, and people running

The general looks at all the chaos

and laughs

"Ya'll act so hard, but clearly ya'll aren't"

The B finds a window and escapes during the generals speech

The block looks around and notices the B's absence

Toughness returns

The same ones that were holding on to each other
    return to their previous state of beefing
    Fear and panic disappear
    and normalcy returns

They Are What They Eat

"I brought a breakfast Mr. Williams"

"That school food is nasty"
So, I ask what you have for breakfast
You open your black plastic bag to reveal:

Flamin Hots (Or Hot Flamins if you're from the southside of Chicago)
    Takis
    Hot Crunchy Curls
    A Superhero Juice
    A few Mambas
    A Zebra Cake
    Winter Fresh Gum

    You then ask if I want something
    I politely respond "No, I don't eat that stuff anymore"
    You ask why?

    Flamin Hots, Takis, and Hot Crunchy Curls all have Red 40 in them

Causing Allergies, hyperactivity, learning impairment, irritability and aggressiveness

And you wonder why you are so mad in the morning

or why you just wanna go off anytime anybody say any random thing to you

Superhero Juice with no real juice in it

It's high fructose corn syrup, sugar, and dye, with a side of water

And you wonder why you don't want to sit down

or why you can't concentrate on your work

Mambas and Zebra Cakes packed with sugar

no real nutritional value

And you wonder why you are still so hungry and your stomach hurts or feel sluggish in class, needing that nap

With Winter Fresh Gum to kill the stench
of food that is designed to kill you

"But my Mama only gave me $2"

"You see all of my stuff together was $2"

"If I buy an apple, that's 89 cent"
"42.5 percent of what I have"
and I can't share it with my friends
and I'm still left hungry
"So what am I supposed to eat?"

Then proceed to eat your "breakfast" with satisfaction

Shortly after
　　You get into a fight about someone taking your line spot
　　Get your mother called
　　She comes to take you home
　　and you return right back to the corner store the very next day
　　To buy the same thing

Frustration Point

How can you tell me about my classroom?
　　When you have only been in it for less than a hour.
　　You don't know the relationships that I've built with students
　　You don't know how things work in here
　　It's like if I went into a dentist office
　　and started telling him that he was pulling teeth wrong
　　like he didn't go to school for this or know his patients

　　How can you tell me about how I interact with students?
　　When you haven't lived in the same neighborhood we both share

You don't know the reason this child is approaching me for a hug

You don't know how a smile might be the only one they got in the last 726 hours

It's like if I walk into Starbucks

and tell the barista that she is being too friendly with the customers

like that isn't her personality or understanding of life

Education is not about the teacher

They don't care about your style or the effect you have on kids

They don't care if you are invested or if you care for them as people and not just numbers

They care about data and compliance

Perception is reality and when you look at me as a black teacher, what do you see?

Am I immediately a pit bull in a yard that you think only lives to bite you
    and bite others...
    Or do I protect the greater good and am actually very friendly and loving

    I'm frustrated because education does not have my back
    Like I have education's back
    It did not fight for me
    Like I fought for it
    It is now a system that seeks to divide and destroy
    While I only seek to reconnect and restore

    I'm frustrated because we all have to experience the trauma of education
    I'm frustrated because I chose to live the trauma all over again

I'm frustrated because no matter how hard I try, I will always be wrong

I'm frustrated because the dreams of changing lives are only meant for white savior education movies

Another Black Male Teacher...

"I don't want you to be another Black Male Teacher" -Principal :(

    I did not comply with orders
    You asked me to send you an assignment
    I did
    It was original, beautiful, and creative
    The kids learned, enjoyed, and loved
    They shared, wrote, and delivered meaningful scripts
    But it was not in the curriculum
    So it was immediately looked down on
    You scolded me about not giving the students what they needed
    Looked down on me about venturing to the outside of Curriculumland
    Then responded
    "You have so much potential"
    "I don't want you to be another stereotypical Black male teacher..."

Sigh

Like you would have any percent of knowledge about what that means

Like you would know what is takes for me to wake up every morning

Like you would know the affect that I have and what effect is had on me

What is a stereotypical black male teacher anyway?

One who teaches away from dead standards and into lives?

One who recognizes needs and allows the students to be themselves?

One who doesn't want the students to comply, but to create their own rules?

No Wonder Black Male Teachers are Non Existent

"They are not used to having young teachers, they are definitely not used to having black teachers, even more rare is a young black teacher. They are not used to that..." (MarKeira, 2017)

Man Syndrome

"You have a man syndrome, you just think you can do whatever you want"
- Principal :(

Oh female principal
    How interesting is our dynamic
    You an old black woman
    Me a younger black man
    Willie Lynch once wrote about us hating each other
    And this you found to be true

    You expect me to be strong, but compliant
    Like a bull that you keep in a cage
    Me expecting you to believe in me and support me
    Like an older church woman to a young minister

So you as my boss believe I should do as I am told

You tell me I have potential, like I'm not already great

You tell me to just follow the game plan

Never thinking I might be writing a new one

So, now I have a man syndrome

I think I can just do whatever I want...

I can just imagine a mind trapped slave said this to a freeman

A black store owner to a protestor

An older black mother to a young black teen who is driving

We are so busy focusing on compliance,

that we forget true education was created for the opposite

I do not seek to threaten your dominance or challenge your throne

At least not intentionally
But that is your biggest subconscious worry

Why don't you get that I want to honor you, Black woman.
So please honor and respect me
Are we so focused on pulling each other down
To feel a slight glimpse of dominance

Black women, please love us, and we love you
We honor your opinion
But do not imprison me in them
For I am a freeman

Last thing...

Do not scold me for being free and happy

Do not tell me I should not create more for students

Do not look to make me compliant

Please...Black Sister

I'm begging you

To not hate me for being a man in education

Won't Be Teaching Long

If you are reading this…
  Then it's probably too late
and
    Your school year has probably gone better than mines
    Far better
    I know that we think black people are supposed to take pain and punishment
    But this is different
    I have gone through everything under the sun
    To stop me from teaching
    and it has almost worked too.
    I mean from student's parents fighting against me,
      to DCFS being called by me and on me,
      to students lying every chance they get to avoid trouble,

to investigations about these lies,
to Admin washing their hands from me because I got too dirty

I've been through huge classrooms
being expected to produce huge results too soon
When I think about it
I was set up to fail,
Told that a black male teacher can fix any problem
Given too many students
Students that "really need a black man to get them back in line"
Given parents that would rather fight me than with me
People that will literally twist every word

Until I wish they heard none

I stayed with my class, but maybe that wasn't the smartest move
Like I wonder if my father ever thought that
Like you're bad if you leave on the kids
but can you be even worse if you stay and hate it
In the beginning of the year I had a parent tell me:
"You have ____,_____, _____, and _____ in the same class?"
"You Won't Be Teaching Long"

I realize that I am here for a reason
And that I will move mountains so sometimes I will get hit with rocks
or boulders
Realize that I will be tested every day
I don't ask for sympathy

I'm a black man who is not supposed to get any
But I just want you to understand
Why I won't be teaching long

Where's The Justice?

Mark 6:4

    But Jesus said unto them, A prophet is not without honour, but in his own country, and among his own kin, and in his own house.

Where is the Justice?
    For a Black Male Teacher
    Like who realistically protects teachers

    from disrespect
Like students cursing at you
and everybody else cursing your name
If you go off, you'll be on the news

    from harm
    Like students taking swings and throwing things at you

and everybody else swinging and throwing things at your name

If you swing back, you'll be on the news

from lies

Like students and admin saying you did something you did not do

and everybody else going along with it

If you lie back, you are not practicing good moral character

Where is the Justice for the teachers?

Like how many times should a student be allowed to disrespect you?

How many times should a parent be allowed to make threats of harm?

How many times should you have to defend yourself in front of admin from lies?

From 8:45 - 3:45 you deal with these things with no legal shield.

Where is the protection?

Or should I wait until burnout?

Or should I wait until a better school has an opening?

Or should I wait until I end up on the news?

Brown Eyes Watching

Brown eyes staring into brown eyes
    We have walked some of the same roads
    but you look pretty unfamiliar
    Eye see compassion
    struggle
    hate
    adoration
    self worth
    self adoration
    You see a teacher
    a traitor
    a hero
    a villain
    someone who doesn't care enough
    someone who cares too much
    someone doing too much
    Your brown eyes are watching
    My brown eyes are watching too
    I know eye cannot slip
    Heroes ledge laced with cocoa butter

Eye can not be wrong
Take an off day because the sub will surely cry
Eye see future success
You see a long road
It took me a long time to be able to see out your eyes
But there are no other eyes that eyed rather be staring in

209 Tunes
part two

We turn our Spotify playlist on again

    Next song to play is the Charade by De'Angelo
    The students sit quietly during the song
    Knowing that it is one of my therapeutic songs
    Not understanding the lyrics
    Or what a charade it is to teach white systematic oppression clothed as education
    and be black at the same time

    Followed by Really Love by De' Angelo again
    I don't think the students understand how really in love with them I am
    The song relaxes them as they work on assignments

"Can we make a request" wakes me from those tears

Say Goodbye by Chris Brown is their request
They jam out like they were auditioning for Breezy
Harmonizing as a class while they are singing
Bringing Harmony to the room
Bringing togetherness to their unity
I am saddened, next year I won't be apart of this unity
"And I know its hard and it's killing me"
There's Never a right time to say Goodbye

To lighten the mood, next plays
Pupil/ The Patience by The Internet

They are learning from me, Pupils
I am learning from them, The Patience
The Pupils dance in their seats to the drum beat
The Patience dances to their work
Bringing Peace and Poise to the room

Black Male Teaching Commercial

There's a black male teacher on a certain commercial
   who is singing,
     dancing,
     and rapping for the students
   He uses his new product to draw cool graffiti figures for students
   The product even comes with a stylus pen
   The marketing is really cool

   But it makes me wonder how the rest of the world sees black male teachers
   Are we supposed to be singing to our students?
   Is that the avenue that we need to express ourselves.

Are we supposed to be dancing when teaching students?

Having them come up with dance moves to remember solutions.

Are we supposed to be rapping for students?

Hoping that they see our words as poetry for a lesson.

In a way I am jealous of this "commercial black male teacher"

he doesn't have to deal with Common Core State Standards

he doesn't have to deal with students who might need more than a song and dance

he is able to be "free" in whatever way he can

Is this what people see when they see a black male teacher?

I mean I sing and dance, but not to sell products

Can we show black males actually teaching?

or does every black man have to look like they are on youtube

even if they are dressed in a suit and tie

even if they are in a classroom.

Honesty Break

I should be honest
    If you thought that Black Males could save education
    You were wrong
    This might be self doubt or tiredness of the system talking
    But this is definitely not designed for us
    Although we built the pyramids
    we are not allowed to create curriculum or even change it
    Although we might smile and be nice to everyone
    we are around people who speak ill of us
    We have intense amount of paper loads
    To match our intense stress load
    We are appreciated only in physicality
    We are not supported because we should not need help
    We are tired
    We want students to learn

    But its hard to move forward and
backwards at the same time
    We are looked at to be snake charmers
    With snakes that have no charm
    Heroes
Where villains rule the land

Ya'll The Reason Why I'm Sick

I've been sick four times in three months
    My immune system has begun to take a hit
    because of yall

    All the times where you've unprotectedly sneezed around me, only to be served with a tissue and "God Bless you"
    All the times where you've shown up to school sick because your parent works and you can't stay home
    All the times where you've thrown up in the hallway, but stated that you were good

All the times where you've coughed with no hand over you while we are in small groups or I am working independently with you

All the times where you've sat at my desk sick because you wanted to see the board closer

or maybe it might be

All the times where I've wiped faces because you forgot to wash that part

All the times where I've hugged crying students with snot running

All the times where I've touched head, praying for you without you knowing

All the times where I've high fived students who got an answer right

All the times where I've dapped you up every time you walk in the classroom

All the times where I've shared my breakfast with you because you didn't have anything

All the times where I've shook your hand because you wanted to show me a new handshake

You are Eleven, But We Expect You to be 31

At your house
    you wake and
    get ready for school in the morning
    There is no smell of breakfast in the air
    You brush your teeth with your batman or frozen toothbrush
    You wash up and
    Begin getting your siblings ready for school
    While getting the door for mom who just finished her overnight shift
    you usher mom to the bed
    grab a few bananas for your siblings and
    head out to school
    Walking with your siblings, catching snowflakes on your tongue, you arrive
    We immediately put you in a line

Tell you to stand correctly and to not talk
You see your best friend and remember you didn't talk to them because
your phone is off
So you begin to say hi
be human
be 11
but you are immediately reprimanded
"If you wanted to talk, you should've done so at home"
"This place is for learning, not talking"
classic teacher script, but you are quiet

We then sit you in a classroom
It's 9 am, but you can't tell because the stale fluorescent lights are on
plus the shades are closed
We remind you again not to talk
but you have to use the bathroom
must be those snowflakes

you ask and are immediately told no
you begin to pout
a very eleven reaction
but you are then reprimanded again
"If you are going to do this, I'm going to call your mother"
you know that she is tired and doesn't want to deal with this
but you feel cheated
"I only asked to go to the bathroom, dang"
The whole class gets quiet
"you must think i'm playing"
ring, ring, ring
Your mother answers and is prepped by the teacher
You are then handed the phone and have your ear filled with expletives, downgrading conversation, and threats
Just the way that she learned

You then try and explain your side to her
but she is not having it
threatening
"if this teacher calls again, I'm going to come up there and embarrass you"
"you're 11 years old, you should be more mature"
"you know I don't play, you there acting like you are grown"

"don't----make------me-----come-----up-----there"

You look at the teacher with tears in your eyes
knowing that you are done for either now or later
"I don't know what those tears are for"
"act more mature"

Black Unicorn

I am a black unicorn
    Rarely seen in time or space
    Rarely heard when trotting about
    or talking
    Hooves untamed by horseshoes
    Man unriddled by a lasso or saddle
    I am a black unicorn
    unable to be trapped

    Yet you want me for two things:

    - To Cut My Horn Off and Wear it as Your Own

    A symbol of triumph and luxury

    1. To Keep Tamed as your Pet

    A symbol of ownership and how rare your collection is

    You despise me for running freely

    Instead demanding that I walk
    slowly enough for you to keep pace with
    Demanding that I be tamed
    Not wanting me to grow too big in size
    You wait to catch me lacking and capture me
    Hoping I will accept the gracious stable that you trap me in
    So that you can feed me hay
    Forgetting that I got my size from God's Green Earth
    You want to ride me with your weight, burdening my bones
    And use me for the labor
    So I cut my horn off
    Share my fur
    Try to blend in with horses
    But as Simba was still a lion
    I am a Black Unicorn
    The only trace you will see of me

Is the gold manure that I leave behind

End of the Year

It is the end of the year
    and you can feel the excitement

the anxiousness

the uneasiness

Kids who hate that the school year is ending

Teachers relieved to free the students

whom they struggled with

created new data about

warned others about

The day ends and everyone is anxious

Students ready to leave

and ready to test someone else

who know you just as well as they know themselves

You know how hard they worked to get to that very position

How hard they studied

acted white

acted like they were the toughest in the room

Just for the opportunity to be in front of the next one in your place

To counter they don't know how hard you've worked

How hard you faked to like the even the worst student

How much trauma you have been through

How much you have cheated and grinded

Just for the opportunity to be in front of them

The bell rings

and the struggle ends

Ashe

Made in the USA
Lexington, KY
15 March 2018